FROM EARTH TO THE STARS

THE EARLY DAYS OF SPACE EXPLORATION

DANIEL E. HARMON

Britannica Educational Publishing
IN ASSOCIATION WITH
ROSEN
EDUCATIONAL SERVICES

Published in 2018 by Britannica Educational Publishing (a trademark of Encyclopædia Britannica, Inc.) in association with The Rosen Publishing Group, Inc., 29 East 21st Street, New York, NY 10010

Distributed exclusively by Rosen Publishing.
To see additional Britannica Educational Publishing titles, go to rosenpublishing.com.

First Edition

Britannica Educational Publishing
J.E. Luebering: Executive Director, Core Editorial
Andrea R. Field: Managing Editor, Compton's by Britannica

Rosen Publishing
Kathy Kuhtz Campbell: Senior Editor
Nelson Sá: Art Director
Brian Garvey: Series Designer
Greg Tucker: Book Layout
Cindy Reiman: Photography Manager
Karen Huang: Photo Researcher

Library of Congress Cataloging-in-Publication Data

Names: Harmon, Daniel E., author.
Title: The early days of space exploration / Daniel E. Harmon
Description: New York : Britannica Educational Publishing : In association with Rosen Educational Services, 2018. | Series: From Earth to the stars | Audience: Grades 5-8. | Includes bibliographical references and index.
Identifiers: LCCN 2016057938 | ISBN 9781680486674 (library bound : alk. paper) | ISBN 9781680486650 (pbk. : alk. paper) | ISBN 9781680486667 (6-pack : alk. paper)
Subjects: Astronomy--History--Juvenile literature. Outer space--Exploration--Juvenile literature.
Classification: LCC QB46 .H2188 2018 | DDC 520.9--dc23

Manufactured in the United States of America

Photo credits: Cover, pp. 1, 35 Bettmann/Getty Images; cover and back cover (background) nienora/Shutterstock.com; pp. 5, 10, 18 © Photos.com/Jupiterimages; p. 8 Science Source; p. 12 Ashmolean Museum, University of Oxford, UK/Bridgeman Images; p. 15 Jay M. Pasachoff/Science Faction/Getty Images; p. 16 De Agostini Picture Library/De Agostini/Getty Images; p. 17 Science & Society Picture Library/Getty Images; pp. 23, 37, 38 Sovfoto/Universal Images Group/Getty Images; p. 25 Science Photo Library/Getty Images; p. 27 SERSeanCrane/Flickr/flickr.com/photos/7196446@N06/407930513/CC BY-SA 2.0; p. 28 Library of Congress, Washington, DC (digital id. ppmsca 02545); p. 30 Marshall Space Flight Center/NASA; p. 32 MSFC/NASA; p. 33 Hulton Archive/Archive Photos/Getty Images; p. 40 NASA/JPL; interior pages graphic pp. 7, 14, 22, 29, 36 Hallowedland/Shutterstock.com.

Contents

Introduction 4

Chapter 1
What's Up There? 7

Chapter 2
A Revolution in Sky Gazing 14

Chapter 3
Into the Modern Era 22

Chapter 4
Reaching Upward 29

Chapter 5
Survival in Space 36

Glossary 42
For Further Reading 44
Index 46

INTRODUCTION

Pathways from Earth to the stars began to be charted thousands of years ago. Stargazers in ancient civilizations were mesmerized by the night skies. Early scientists began recording notes of what they saw, or thought they were seeing. The science of astronomy—the scholarly examination of objects and phenomena in outer space—began in these ancient cultures. The word itself comes from two Greek words meaning "star" (*astron*) and "to name" (*nemein*).

Philosophers and writers penned musings of what it might be like to fly above Earth and visit the stars. They envisioned aerial warfare among the gods of their cultures. Some of their myths were handed down through the centuries. A classic tale is that of Daedalus and Icarus.

In Greek mythology, Daedalus was an inventor and sculptor whose work led to dangerous entanglements with gods and human royalty. He and his son, Icarus, were imprisoned by an angry king inside a complex labyrinth. To escape, Daedalus made them wings consisting of feathers bound by wax. Daedalus flew to freedom, but Icarus flew too high, approaching the sun. The heat melted his wings and he fell to his death.

This legend is one of many age-old stories referring to spaceflight. Writings in different societies told of flying machines and voyages to other worlds.

No serious efforts were made to convert such fantasies to reality. The necessary materials and technology simply did not exist. Humans had no way to propel themselves

The first piloted gas balloon, launched in 1783, did not come close to the edge of space, but it was a milestone in the history of flight.

upward except to jump or climb. So for many centuries, their studies of the upper realms were limited to visual observations. Using only the naked eye and primitive instruments of measurement, early scientists studied the sun, moon, star constellations, and first known planets. They wrote down their findings. They formed theories—usually flawed—about the motions and relationships of heavenly bodies.

Then came the telescope. Beginning in the early 1600s, astronomers were able to view cosmic objects "close up." The enlargements were not at all great by modern standards, but they were astonishing at the time. New knowledge helped correct and clarify old notions about how the universe functions. Telescopes were steadily improved, and new tools were introduced.

The first successes in actually probing the heights occurred more than two hundred years ago. Experimenters first leveraged wind power to fly kites. Beginning in the 1780s, balloons filled with hot air or lighter-than-air gases such as hydrogen and helium were sent higher and higher into the skies. The first piloted balloon flight was made in 1783.

The great breakthrough in the quest to explore space was the invention of the powered airplane in the early twentieth century. After that, the ultimate objective of space scientists was tantalizingly within reach: manned flights above Earth's atmosphere.

CHAPTER 1

WHAT'S UP THERE?

The earliest humans, gazing into night skies dotted with white specks, must have wondered: *What's up there?* Every generation since then has asked the same question.

Over the centuries, dedicated astronomers have accumulated an immense body of knowledge about the solar system and the immeasurable space beyond. Still they probe. New discoveries are made every day. It is obvious, though, that the puzzle of the stars can never be completely understood. When studying the universe, questions that are finally answered present new mysteries.

EARLY ASTRONOMERS

The earliest sophisticated astronomy arose in ancient Babylonia. Babylonian scholars believed the universe existed on six levels. The surface of Earth was one level, the visible stars above it another level. They believed two additional levels of heaven existed above the visible sky and two underworlds existed beneath Earth's surface.

A stone tablet more than two thousand years old preserves records of Babylonian sky watchers' observations of the planet Venus.

The powerful Babylonian civilization was centered in what is now southern Iraq during the eighteenth to sixth centuries BCE. Although their conception of the universe proved wrong, they contributed to the science of astronomy. They made detailed records of the positions of prominent heavenly bodies and devised calendars based on their observations.

The ancient Greeks were not as advanced in astronomy as the Babylonians. They made a breakthrough,

THE FIRST "PREDICTIVE" SCIENCE

Using night-by-night observations recorded over many years, ancient Babylonian astronomers achieved the ability to predict the behavior of the moon and the planets. Their work was important in the development of astronomy as one of the earliest sciences. The Babylonians also applied their observations to a pseudoscience—astrology. Astrologists believe that the motions and positions of celestial objects affect events on Earth. The Babylonians studied the skies largely because they thought the gods sent signs from heaven to warn the king about such events as impending war, a bad barley harvest, or an impending epidemic.

Most scientists scoff at astrology. But until recent centuries, astrology was considered part of astronomy. Astronomers advised nobles of coming events based on astrological calculations. The scientists might not have believed in astrology themselves—but they needed the money they were paid.

A seventeenth-century mapmaker's diagram illustrates Ptolemy's idea that the other known planets orbited around Earth.

however, in applying geometry to their observations of the night skies. The early Greek astronomers knew many of the geometric relationships of the heavenly bodies.

Among the most important Greek scientists were Eudoxus (about 395–342 BCE), Aristotle (384–322 BCE), and Ptolemy (about 100–170 CE). Eudoxus believed Earth was at the center of the universe and did not move. Aristotle realized that Earth is shaped roughly like a ball—which explained its circular shadow across the moon during lunar eclipses. Ptolemy agreed with them. He developed the idea, based on mathematical calculations, that the known planets orbited Earth. He explained his theory in *Mathematike Syntaxis* (The Mathematical Arrangement), also called *Almagest* (an Arabic corruption of the Greek word for "greatest").

These early astronomers identified the most clearly visible planets, including Mars and Venus, as well as star groups. Observations of the planets' motions had a profound impact on their primitive understanding of the solar system. Most of the theories they formed, though, were incorrect.

THE FIRST TOOLS OF SPACE EXPLORERS

The first astronomers cannot be faulted for drawing erroneous conclusions from the observations they made. Lacking instruments of magnification, they saw only what the naked eye revealed. They did have certain important instruments, however, and they learned to make excellent use of them.

The Greeks invented the astrolabe. This device was a disk marked along the edges with degrees of the circle and

A brass figure made in India in the eighteenth century depicts a mounted warrior carrying rocket launchers.

with movable pointers. It was used to determine the angular distance between points in the sky and to compare the positions of the planets or the moon to fixed stars.

Chinese inventors are credited with making the first rockets in the thirteenth century. Historians speculate that early Chinese rockets basically were bamboo tubes attached to arrows and propelled by gunpowder. Simple rocketry spread to Arabia and Europe.

Rockets at first were used as weapons of war and as fireworks. In the twentieth century, modern scientists would use powerful rockets in space exploration.

CHAPTER 2

A REVOLUTION IN SKY GAZING

Science historians consider the sixteenth, seventeenth, and early eighteenth centuries the period of the Scientific Revolution in Europe. It is called a "revolution" because profound new theories and discoveries led to a rethinking of long-standing assumptions.

Among the most famous astronomers and mathematicians of those centuries were Nicolaus Copernicus, Galileo Galilei, and Isaac Newton. Many other scholars also contributed fresh knowledge and ideas.

ASTRONOMERS GATHER EXTRAORDINARY NEW INFORMATION

Until then, practically all astronomers assumed Ptolemy was right about Earth being the center of the universe. This concept is called a geocentric—Earth-centered—model of the universe. In the 1500s, a few scientists began to suspect the sun is the center, with Earth and other planets revolving around it.

The sun-centered view is known as the heliocentric model of the universe. Mounting evidence by different observers during the Scientific Revolution was introduced to support it.

NICOLAUS COPERNICUS

Copernicus (1473–1543) was raised by a wealthy uncle who sent him to excellent schools. While a student at the University of Kraków in the 1490s, he became absorbed in mathematics and astronomy.

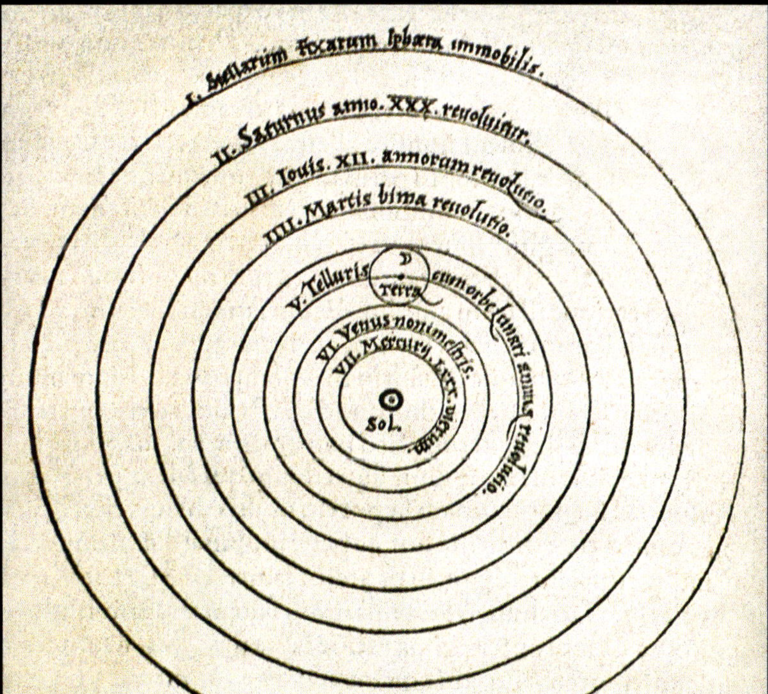

Nicolaus Copernicus put forth his sun-centered (heliocentric) model of the universe in a book published in 1543.

After careful study, Copernicus hit upon the revolutionary idea that Earth and the other planets revolve around the sun. His theory was so controversial, however, that he delayed its publication until 1543, the year of his death.

GALILEO GALILEI

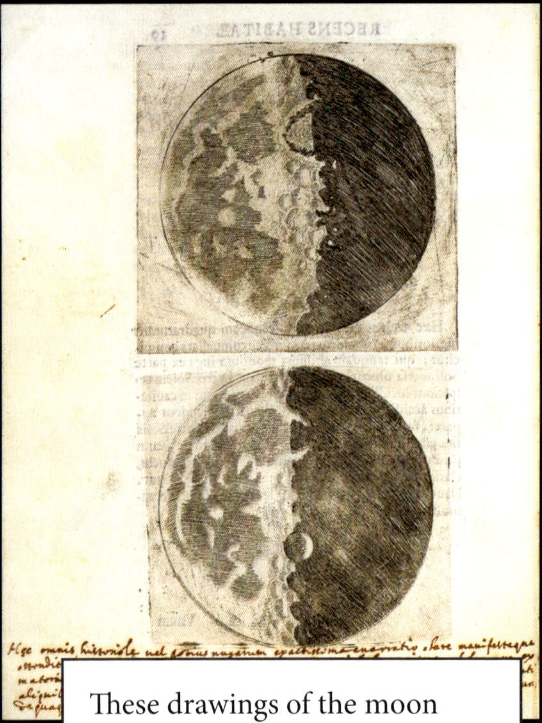

These drawings of the moon appeared in Galileo Galilei's *Sidereus Nuncius* (*The Starry Messenger*), published in 1610. Galileo was one of the first astronomers to use telescopes to observe the heavens.

Galileo Galilei (1564–1642) was born in Italy. Before he was twenty years old, he made an important discovery in physics. His calculations of pendulum swings were vital in making accurate timekeeping devices.

In astronomy, Galileo was one of the first to use a telescope. He greatly improved on earlier models and used it to make important observations of the planets. He embraced the teachings of Copernicus.

TYCHO BRAHE AND JOHANNES KEPLER

Tycho Brahe (1546–1601) of Denmark studied law before turning to astronomy in the

An engraving depicts Tycho Brahe, in the center with arm upraised, and the work of his observatory, called Uraniborg.

1560s. He was a pioneer in developing astronomical instruments and in measuring the positions of the stars and planets. His observations were the most accurate possible before the invention of the telescope.

Johannes Kepler (1571–1630), a German, taught mathematics before he was appointed as Tycho's leading assistant in 1600. When Tycho died the following year, Kepler inherited Tycho's position as court mathematician to Holy Roman emperor Rudolf II as well as his observational data.

Kepler wrote numerous books, some of which became classic studies in astronomy. In *Epitome Astronomiae Copernicanae* (1618–1621; *Epitome of Copernican Astronomy*), Kepler explained his three laws describing how planets move in their orbits around the sun. In 1627, he published *Tabulae Rudolphinae* (Rudolphine Tables), containing planetary tables and a star catalog based mainly on Tycho's observations.

SIR ISAAC NEWTON

Sir Isaac Newton was a prominent leader of the Scientific Revolution. He is noted especially for establishing the basic laws of gravitation and motion.

The leading innovator at the end of the Scientific Revolution was English physicist and mathematician Sir Isaac Newton (1642–1727). He formulated three laws of motion that are the basic principles of modern physics. He was also one of the developers of the branch of mathematics called calculus.

Newton's laws of motion led to his formulation of the law of universal gravitation. This law provided a new

GRAVITY'S "ATTRACTIVE" CHALLENGE

The first challenge in spaceflight is finding a way to break free of Earth's gravity. In the late 1500s, Galileo made the earliest scientific studies of this invisible force. He showed that objects of different sizes fall at the same speed. Until then, people assumed heavier objects fall faster.

Sir Isaac Newton applied theories of gravity to objects in space. He came up with the law of universal gravitation. Newton explained how gravity is the force that keeps planets in orbit around the sun (instead of breaking away and flying off into space). Likewise, it keeps the moon revolving around Earth.

Understanding the force of Earth's gravitational attraction with mathematical precision is essential to modern space scientists. For example, it enables them to determine how much thrust is required to launch a rocket of a certain weight and design into the air, and how far it will go.

explanation of motions of Earth and its moon, as well as the movements of other planets and their moons. It had a profound impact on scientists' understanding of outer space.

OTHER HISTORIC SPACE EXPLORERS

Those famous scientists were not the only ones to make important discoveries about the cosmos during the Scientific Revolution and in the following centuries. Hundreds of scholars were studying the movements of the planets, comets, and other space objects and phenomena.

In England, Edmond Halley (1656–1742) was the first to calculate the orbit of a comet around the sun. He correctly predicted that a certain comet would reappear sixteen years after his death; that comet now bears his name. William Herschel (1738–1822), a German who immigrated to England, made remarkable findings with the large telescopes he designed and improved. He discovered the planet Uranus in 1781.

French astronomer Charles Messier (1730–1817) recorded the existence of more than one hundred star clusters, nebulae, and galaxies. Johann Gottfried Galle (1812–1910) of Germany identified Neptune—at that time the farthest known planet—in 1846.

BRINGING CELESTIAL OBJECTS UP CLOSE

Around 1600, several European eyeglass makers began experimenting with ways not just to improve a person's vision but also to magnify distant objects. In 1608, Hans Lippershey (1570–1619) of the Netherlands made some of the first primitive telescopes. His design called for viewing through two separate lenses. One lens was concave, curved slightly inward like the inside of a bowl. The other was convex, curved outward like a ball. Lippershey called his device a *kijker*—"looker."

A year later, Galileo Galilei used Lippershey's ideas to begin making his own telescopes. These early telescopes were crude. Galileo's first devices could make objects appear only three times larger than they appeared to the naked eye.

He eventually improved magnification to thirty-three times. Still, the objects were blurry and the lighting poor.

Johannes Kepler suggested an important improvement: using two convex lenses. After his death, the Keplerian telescope proved to be a major innovation. It allowed for higher magnification and clearer viewing.

Another advance occurred in 1668. Sir Isaac Newton designed and built what is called a reflecting telescope. This type uses mirrors instead of lenses to collect and focus light rays. A great advantage is the elimination of distortion that occurs in refracting (lens-based) telescopes, which results in clearer images.

The telescope was the most important invention for studying the night skies. Soon, scientists were able to detect countless details of the solar system that their predecessors had missed.

CHAPTER 3

INTO THE MODERN ERA

In the late nineteenth and early twentieth centuries, a number of scientists began taking major steps toward turning theories of space exploration into reality. During this period, several individuals and groups from a number of countries worked to solve the theoretical and technical problems of space travel.

Distinguished theorists of the era included Russian research scientist Konstantin E. Tsiolkovsky (1857–1935) and German physicist Hermann Oberth (1894–1989). One was physically impaired and rose from a modest upbringing. The other was the son of a wealthy doctor and seemed destined to become a scientist.

TSIOLKOVSKY AND OBERTH

Konstantin E. Tsiolkovsky was stricken with scarlet fever when he was nine. He survived, but it left him nearly deaf. Throughout his life, he had to rely on an ear trumpet.

Tsiolkovsky obtained his early education at home. He immersed himself in books and became keenly interested in math and science. Perhaps inspired by popular science fiction novels such as Jules Verne's *From the Earth to the Moon* (1865), he began to wonder if spaceflight was really possible.

After studying science in Moscow, Tsiolkovsky began teaching while pursuing his scientific interests. He developed ideas concerning gases and other subjects that brought him to the notice of leading Russian scientists.

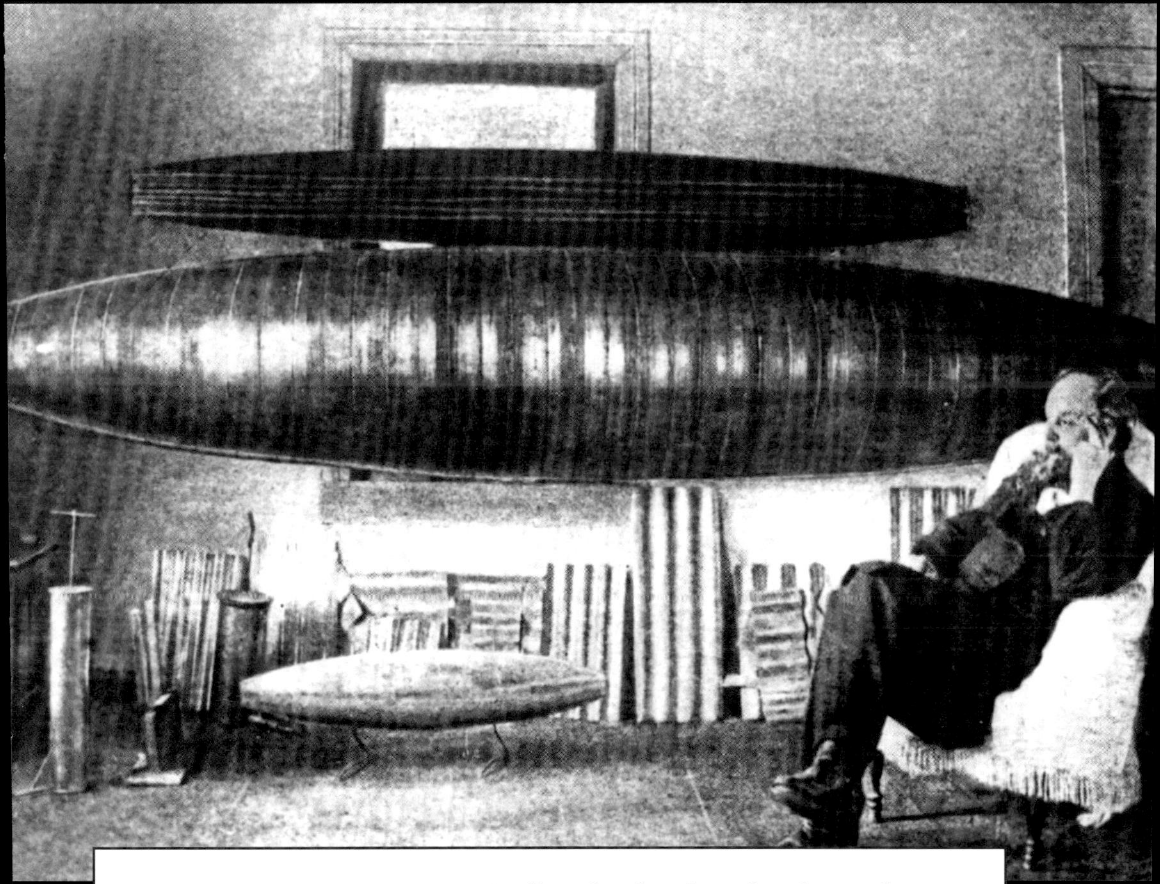

Russian scientist Konstantin Tsiolkovsky developed and tested important ideas about rocketry. He is shown here in his workshop.

FIRST LADY OF ASTRONOMY

Sir William Herschel, a German-born English astronomer, earned his place in history by identifying the planet Uranus in 1781. Less well known, but no less important in the progress of space studies, was his sister. Caroline Lucretia Herschel (1750–1848) recorded careful notes and did many of the calculations connected with her brother's studies. She went on to contribute extensive records to the growing scientific catalog of stars.

William and Caroline relocated from their native Germany to England, where William became a music teacher. His passion, though, was astronomy. In 1782, he was appointed official court astronomer to King George III. Caroline at first served as little more than William's housekeeper. Gradually, she assumed the task of making detailed calculations to support his work.

Caroline began studying the skies herself, using a small reflecting telescope. King George recognized her usefulness and gave her a salary of her own while she worked with her brother.

In the coming years, Caroline edited and organized catalogs of stars. For her painstaking work, the Royal Astronomical Society awarded her a gold medal—an extraordinary honor for a woman of the time.

Cataloging the findings of others was not her only contribution to astronomy. Caroline Herschel is credited with discovering eight comets and three nebulae. One of the comets is named after her.

Caroline Herschel assisted her astronomer brother, William, while also earning recognition in her own right for her observations of comets and other heavenly objects.

Tsiolkovsky became consumed with the idea of building a metal dirigible (airship), which might be controlled better than those made of fabric. To test his ideas, he built a wind tunnel. He studied the effects of air resistance on objects passing through it.

Tsiolkovsky turned his attention increasingly to the possibility of space travel. His work dealt with theoretical problems of using rocket engines in space, including heat transfer, a navigating mechanism, and maintenance of fuel supply.

Hermann Oberth's father was a respected physician. Hermann himself studied to be a doctor, but World War I (1914–1918) disrupted his plans. He joined the Austro-Hungarian army and was wounded in battle. It freed him to resume his studies. He now focused on astronautics.

Oberth, like Tsiolkovsky and other visionaries, believed manned space missions were possible. He conducted experiments about the state of weightlessness and came up with a design for a long-range rocket propelled by flammable chemical liquids. In 1923, Oberth's book *Die Rakete zu den Planetenräumen* (*The Rocket into Interplanetary Space*) was published. It proposed ideas for how rockets could propel manned spaceflights beyond Earth's gravity.

NEW INVENTIONS

While brilliant theories were being developed and refined, practical observations and experiments were advancing the quest for the stars. Old scientific tools were improved, and new ones were invented.

Several American colleges and universities built powerful observatories during the 1800s, such as the Hopkins Observatory at Williams College in Massachusetts.

Observations of the sun are important in space science. The spectroheliograph, used to photograph the sun, was invented in 1889. It was followed by similar instruments such as the coronagraph. This type of telescope blocks sunlight so that the sun's outer atmosphere, or corona, can be studied.

Otto Lilienthal performed some two thousand daring experiments with winged flight. He was killed in a glider crash in 1896.

Meanwhile, observatories equipped with increas ingly advanced telescopes were built, mainly at colleges anc universities. Notable ones were at Yale University (Atheneum completed in 1830), Williams College (Hopkins Obser vatory, 1838), and the University of Virginia (McCormicl Observatory, 1884).

But the most sensational inventions of the er were the flying machines. Hot-air balloons began carryin people aloft in the 1780s. German engineer Otto Lilientha (1848–1896) experimented extensively with contraption not unlike today's hang gliders—which ultimately resultec in his death. In the United States, the Wright brothers ar credited with making the first controlled, sustained fligh of an engine-powered airplane in 1903. These early aircraf were the ancestors of spaceships.

CHAPTER 4

REACHING UPWARD

By the early twentieth century, space scientists were intent on finding ways to propel aircraft farther and higher. They took seriously Oberth's proposal in *The Rocket into Interplanetary Space* for launching manned aircraft into space.

Many scientists in different countries contributed to the development of space exploration. Notable among them were Robert Goddard and Wernher von Braun.

GODDARD—UNAPPRECIATED PIONEER

Today, the pioneering physicist Robert H. Goddard (1882–1945) is considered by many to be the father of modern rocketry. However, the value of his work went largely unrecognized during his lifetime.

From childhood, Goddard was deeply interested in mechanics, physics, and inventions. When he was sixteen, he read H. G. Wells's classic science fiction novel *The War of the Worlds* (1898). He began to wonder if a spaceship really could be constructed. Twenty years later, he wrote a scientific

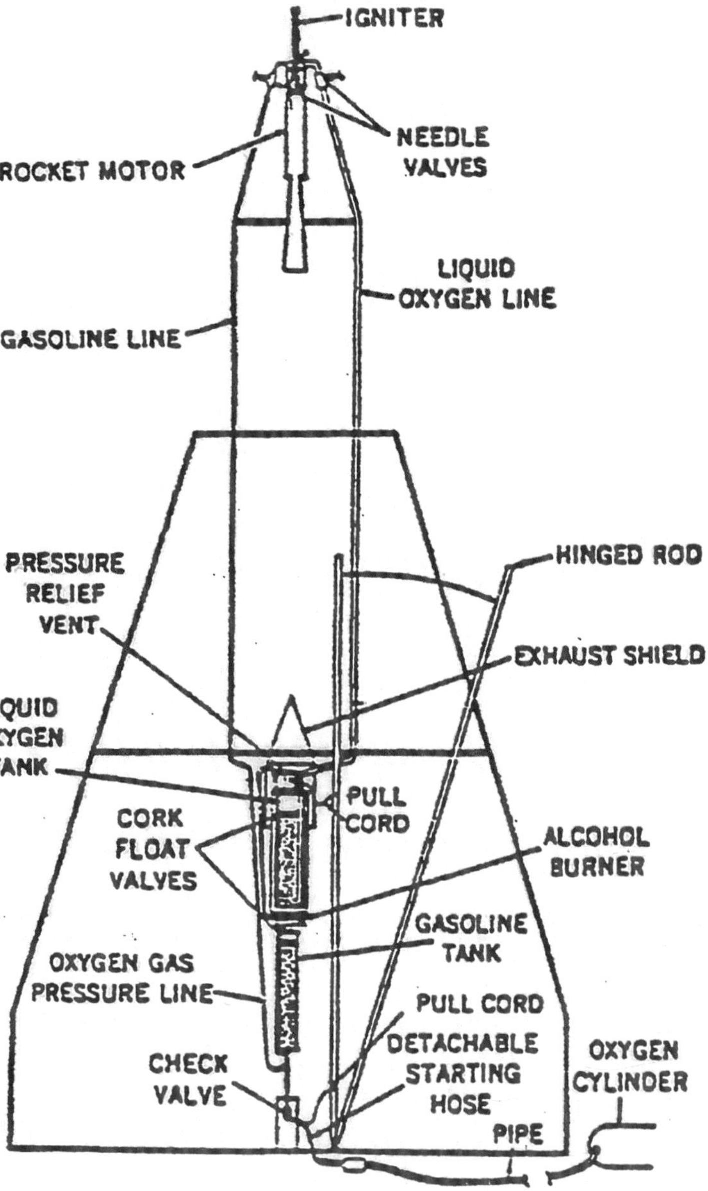

Figure 1
Dr. Goddard's 1926 Rocket

Although Robert Goddard's 1926 rocket, illustrated in this diagram, flew for only 2.5 seconds, it was a milestone in rocket development.

text, *A Method of Reaching Extreme Altitudes* (1919). In it, he suggested that rockets eventually could travel all the way to the moon. He provided mathematical calculations of how much rocket thrust it would take to carry loads of different weights to different altitudes.

While teaching physics at Clark University in Massachusetts, Goddard made vital experiments and calculations in thrust and propulsion. He was the first scientist to make a rocket motor powered by liquid fuel. With liquid fuels, it is easier for engineers to control the intensity of burning than with solid fuels. In March 1926, he launched the world's first successful liquid-fuel rocket on a Massachusetts farm.

With financial backing from wealthy aviation enthusiasts, Goddard set up a small research center in the desert near Roswell, New Mexico. There, in 1935, he was able to propel a liquid-fuel rocket faster than the speed of sound. He developed a rocket steering system and proposed the idea of launching a craft that used multistage, or step, rockets to reach higher altitudes.

The news media gleefully scoffed at "Moony" Goddard who dreamed of travel in space. Within years of his death, though, the US space program took advantage of his innovations.

BRAUN—GERMANY'S GIFT TO THE US SPACE PROGRAM

While Goddard was experimenting with liquid-fuel rockets in the United States, Wernher von Braun (1912–1977) was working along similar lines in Germany. Inspired by the writings of Hermann Oberth, Braun devoted himself to rocket science and earned a PhD degree in physics at age

Wernher von Braun and his team of German scientists came to the United States after World War II and spearheaded the nation's space program.

STRANGE FICTION

Science fiction (sci-fi) has been one of the most popular categories of literature and films for almost a century. *Buck Rogers* and *Flash Gordon* comic strips and radio serials became popular in the 1930s. *Star Wars*, *Star Trek*, *The X-Files*, and other films and television serials have millions of devotees today.

Sci-fi literature actually appeared almost two thousand years ago. Among the works of Plutarch, a writer of ancient Greece, was *On the Face Which Appears on the Orb of the Moon*. Plutarch suggested that the moon was similar to Earth, but smaller. Another Greek, Lucian, wrote *True History* (160). He told of an expedition of sailors caught in a mysterious whirlwind that lifted them all the way to the moon.

During the Scientific Revolution, Johannes Kepler wrote a novel titled *Somnium* (*The Dream*). He wondered how the universe would look if he lived on the moon.

Science fiction literature began to appear on a broad scale in the nineteenth century. Jules Verne's *From the Earth to the Moon* was published in 1865. Verne wrote of three men propelled to the moon by being shot from a large cannon.

Edward Everett Hale's "The Brick Moon" was a short story published in 1869–1870. Hale envisioned an artificial Earth satellite made of bricks. H. G. Wells wrote *The War of the Worlds* (1898). It described an invasion of Earth by Martians.

An illustration from Jules Verne's novel *From the Earth to the Moon* depicts a sectioned rocket traveling to the moon.

twenty-two. During World War II (1939–1945), he was technical director of rocket research and production in Peenemünde, Germany.

Braun and his team developed a long-range rocket, the V-2, which was used against Great Britain during the war. The V-2 was powered by liquid fuel. After the war, American authorities recruited Braun and his associates into the US rocket program. Braun became vital to American efforts in the "space race" against the Soviet Union.

Braun's crowning achievement was directing the development of the Saturn V rocket during the 1960s. The Saturn V lifted Apollo spacecraft from Earth on their missions to the moon.

ROCKET SOCIETIES

Inspired by the work and writings of Tsiolkovsky, Oberth, Goddard, and others, people around the world became fascinated by rocket science during the early 1900s. Amateur hobbyists, joined by professional engineers, bonded in organized rocket societies. Some of the leading space scientists of the twentieth century, including Wernher von Braun, were members of these societies.

Notable societies included the Society for the Study of Interplanetary Travel in the Soviet Union, the Society for Space Travel in Germany, and the American Interplanetary Society in the United States. Some societies were merged into government space programs or grew to become major research institutions.

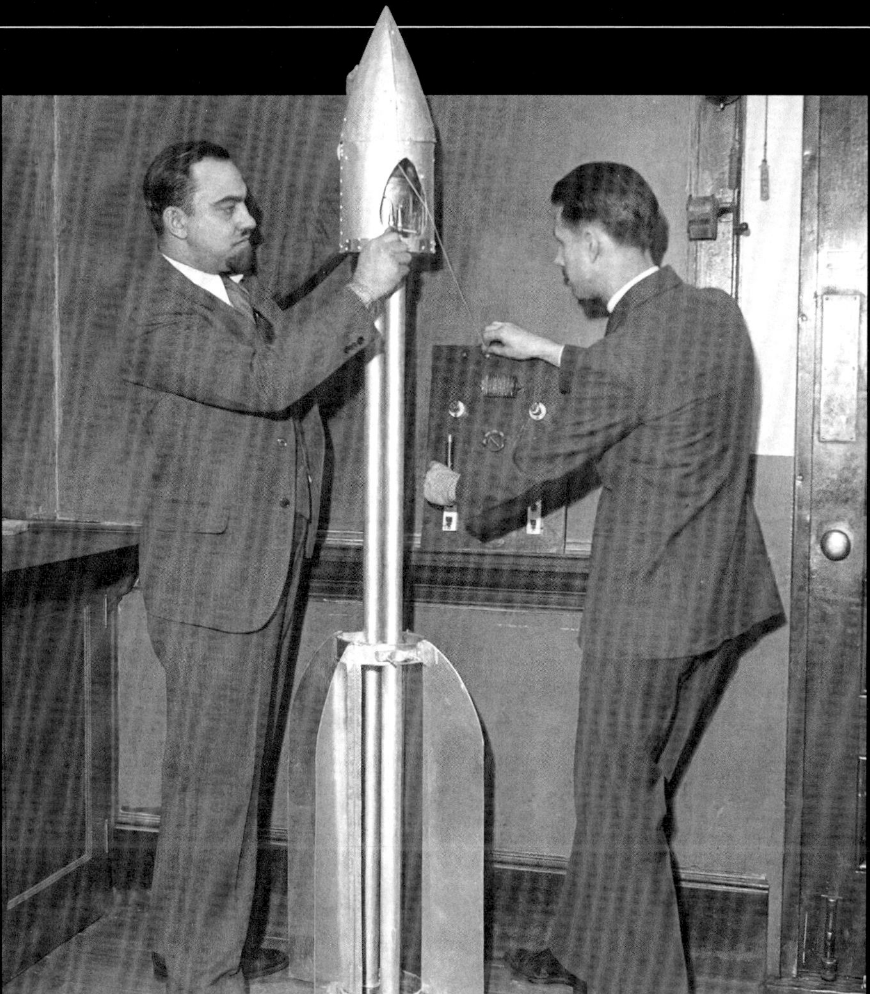

In a photograph from 1932, officials of the American Interplanetary Society demonstrate a device that controls the flow of fuel inside a rocket.

Rocket societies conducted sophisticated experiments. In the mid-1930s, a small group of scholars at the California Institute of Technology conducted particularly dangerous experiments with rocket fuels. They were dubbed the "Suicide Squad."

Chapter 5

Survival in Space

Tsiolkovsky, Goddard, Braun, and others had demonstrated that rockets could break out of Earth's gravity and enter the realm of outer space. The next question was obvious: Could humans be launched into space—and survive?

The American and Russian space programs did not begin seeking the answer by firing up rockets bearing capsules with human daredevils aboard. They first launched animals. They carefully studied the effects on animals of liftoff and of living in a state of weightlessness. Soon after the first successful launch of an artificial satellite into orbit in 1957, government space programs began placing test animals aboard spacecraft. Monitoring apparatus attached to their bodies sent back information about their physical condition, moment by moment.

The frenzied space rivalry between the United States and the Soviet Union was set against the backdrop of the Cold War. After World War II, the two countries emerged as world superpowers. Both were developing nuclear weapons.

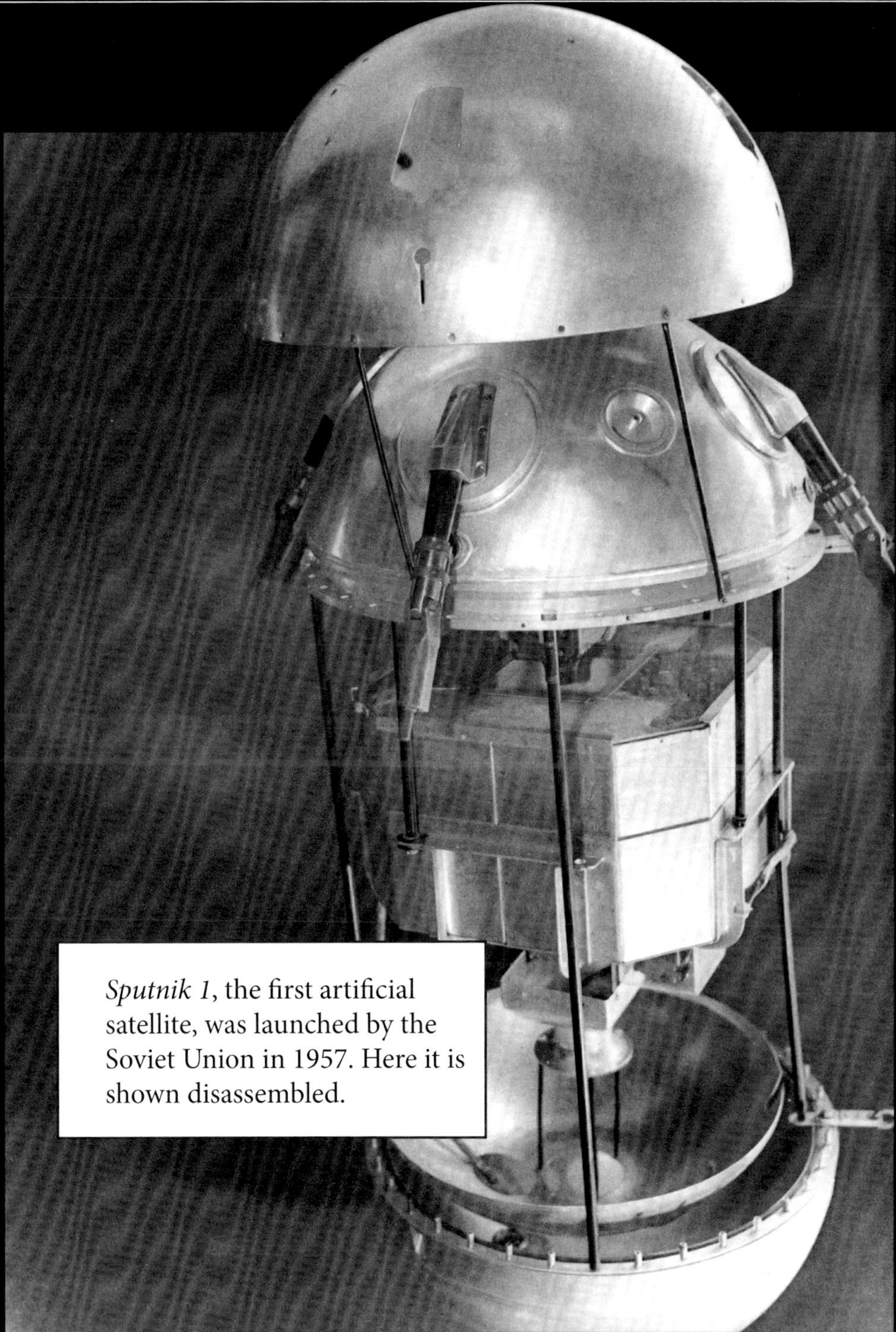

Sputnik 1, the first artificial satellite, was launched by the Soviet Union in 1957. Here it is shown disassembled.

FURRY SPACE MARTYRS

American scientists began sending animals high into the atmosphere during tests in the late 1940s. The first animal to reach the altitude above the atmosphere that is considered outer space was a monkey launched aboard a V-2 rocket in 1949. Many of the early test animals, mainly monkeys and mice, perished. The first animals to live through a test flight were eleven mice and a monkey, Yorick, in 1951.

The first living creature sent into orbit around Earth was a stray dog. Soviet authorities caught a mixed-breed mongrel on the streets of Moscow. They placed her in a capsule and launched her into orbit aboard *Sputnik 2* in November 1957. They named her Laika, which means "Barker" in Russian.

The story of Laika is very sad. The Soviets had no plan for bringing the satellite back to Earth. Laika died in space.

Medical data transmitted back to Earth, however, was valuable in monitoring life-supporting conditions aboard a vessel in space. Years later, Laika received an honor she well deserved. Soviet space officials placed a plaque in her name at the research center in Moscow where she was trained.

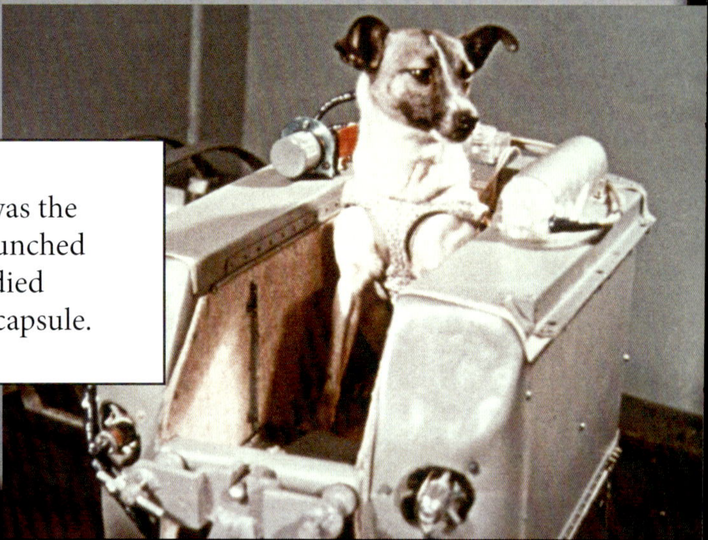

Laika, a female dog, was the first living creature launched into Earth orbit. She died aboard the *Sputnik 2* capsule.

The so-called space race was central to the strategies of both countries during those tense years.

AMERICAN AND SOVIET ACHIEVEMENTS

The Russians initially led the United States in the space race during the 1950s. Their first two sensational triumphs occurred back to back in 1957. The Soviets successfully launched *Sputnik 1*, the first artificial satellite, into orbit around Earth on October 4. On November 3, *Sputnik 2* lifted the first earthling—a stray dog—into orbit. Soon after the success of these missions, the Russians began a more ambitious program: launching vehicles to explore the moon.

The United States was just three months behind in launching its first satellite, *Explorer 1*. Both countries' space programs suffered launchpad explosions, aborted flights, and other failures.

Early satellites such as *Sputnik* and *Explorer* gave scientists valuable data about possible living conditions aboard spacecraft. The ultimate goal, of course, was to send humans into space.

The original Soviet achievements both amazed and alarmed Americans. People worried that Soviet satellites were spying on them. In time, they thought, the Soviets would be able to fire down nuclear warheads from outer space. The US government, in response, stepped up its own space program. American political leaders and scientists did not like being viewed by the world as the runner-up in the space race.

(*From left to right*) William H. Pickering, James A. Van Allen, and Wernher von Braun triumphantly display a model of the *Explorer I* satellite in 1958.

Early Soviet domination had interesting effects on American society. Perhaps most notable was a shift in educational focus. Educational leaders warned that the nation was lagging in space exploration because it was not generating adequate interest in science among its students. Science programs began to be emphasized in public schools.

HUMANS ARRIVE IN THE WEIGHTLESS REALM

On April 12, 1961, the Soviets attained the prize that both world superpowers had labored so long to win. Cosmonaut Yury Gagarin became the first human to be launched into outer space. His capsule orbited Earth once, then reentered the atmosphere and descended beneath parachutes. Gagarin bailed out several miles above the ground and landed unhurt in a field.

American astronauts soon followed. Within a few years, they were setting new flight records that far surpassed those of the Russians. Together, bold American and Soviet pilots led the world into the era of human spaceflight.

GLOSSARY

ASTRONAUTICS Science of building and operating space vehicles.

CALCULUS Form of mathematics dealing with change in processes or systems.

CONSTELLATION Configuration or "dot pattern" formed by selected stars.

COSMOS Universe.

LABYRINTH Maze.

NEBULAE Clouds of gas or dust in space.

NUCLEAR WEAPON Military tools that get their destructive power from the energy that is created when the nuclei of atoms are split apart or joined together.

ORBIT Path of an object as it revolves around another object.

OUTER SPACE Realm of the universe that begins about 62 miles (100 kilometers) above Earth's surface.

PHYSICS Science dealing with matter and energy and their interactions.

PSEUDOSCIENCE System that tries to explain physical phenomena that cannot be proven by the scientific method.

SATELLITE A natural or artificial object that orbits another object.

STAR CLUSTER Hundreds or thousands of stars in a related group.

THRUST Force that pushes an object forward or upward.

WARHEAD The part of a missile that contains the explosive.

For Further Reading

Anderson, Michael, ed. *Pioneers in Astronomy and Space Exploration* (Inventors and Innovators). New York, NY: Britannica Educational Publishing, 2013.

Bortz, Fred. *The Sun-Centered Universe and Nicolaus Copernicus* (Revolutionary Discoveries of Scientific Pioneers). New York, NY: Rosen Publishing, 2014.

Dickmann, Nancy. *Exploring Comets, Asteroids, and Other Objects in Space* (Spectacular Space Science). New York, NY: Rosen Publishing, 2016.

Gilliland, Ben. *Rocket Science for the Rest of Us: Cutting-Edge Concepts Made Simple*. New York, NY: DK Publishing, 2015.

Kazlow, Samuel, ed. *Astronomy: Understanding Celestial Bodies* (The Study of Science). New York, NY: Britannica Educational Publishing, 2015.

Lippincott, Kristen. *Astronomy* (Eyewitness Books). New York, NY: DK Publishing, 2013.

Mallick, Nita, ed. *Space Exploration* (The Study of Science). New York, NY: Britannica Educational Publishing, 2017.

Miller, Ron. *Recentering the Universe: The Radical Theories of Copernicus, Kepler, Galileo, and Newton*. Minneapolis, MN: Twenty-First Century Books, 2014.

Morgan, Ben, ed. *Space!* (Smithsonian Knowledge Encyclopedia). New York, NY: DK Publishing, 2015.

Redfern, Nick. *True Stories of Space Exploration Conspiracies* (Off the Record!). New York, NY: Rosen Publishing, 2015.

WEBSITES

Because of the changing nature of internet links, Rosen Publishing has developed an online list of websites related to the subject of this book. This site is updated regularly. Please use this link to access the list:

http://www.rosenlinks.com/FETTS/early

INDEX

A

airplanes, 6, 28
Almagest, 11
American Interplanetary Society, 34
animals in space, 36, 38
Apollo spacecraft, 34
Aristotle, 11
astrolabe, 11–13
astrology, 9
astronomy, derivation of term, 4
Atheneum, 28

B

Babylonians, 7–9
balloons/balloon flight, 6, 28
Brahe, Tycho, 16–17, 18
Braun, Wernher von, 29, 31–34, 36
"Brick Man, The," 33

C

calculus, 18
California Institute of Technology, 35
Chinese, early rockets, 13
Copernicus, Nicolaus, 14, 15–16
coronagraph, 27

E

Eudoxus, 11
Explorer 1, 39

F

From the Earth to the Moon, 23, 33
fuel, rocket, 31, 34, 35

G

Gagarin, Yury, 41
Galileo Galilei, 14, 16, 19, 20–21
Galle, Johann Gottfried, 20
geocentric model of the universe, 14
geometry, 11
George III, 24
Goddard, Robert, 29–31, 34, 36
Greeks, ancient, 9–11

H

Hale, Edward Everett, 33
Halley, Edmond, 20
heliocentric model of the universe, 15, 16
Herschel, Caroline Lucretia, 24
Herschel, William, 20, 24
Hopkins Observatory, 28

K

Kepler, Johannes, 17–18, 21, 33
Keplerian telescope, 21

L

Laika, 38, 39
Lilienthal, Otto, 28
Lippershey, Hans, 20
liquid fuels, 31, 34
Lucian, 33

M

Mars, 11
McCormick Observatory, 28
Messier, Charles, 20
Method of Reaching Extreme Altitudes, A, 31
motion, laws of, 18

N

Neptune, 20
Newton, Isaac, 14, 18–19, 21

O

Oberth, Hermann, 22, 26, 29, 32, 34
observatories, 28
On the Face Which Appears on the Orb of the Moon, 33

P

Plutarch, 33
Ptolemy, 11, 14

R

reflecting telescopes, 21
refracting telescopes, 21
Rocket into Interplanetary Space, The, 26, 29
rocket societies, 34–35

Royal Astronomical Society, 24
Rudolf II, 18

S

Saturn V rocket, 34
science fiction literature, 33
Scientific Revolution, 14, 15, 18, 19, 33
Society for Space Travel, 34
Society for the Study of Interplanetary Travel, 34
solid fuels, 31
Somnium, 33
space race, 34, 36–39
spectroheliograph, 27
Sputnik 1, 39
Sputnik 2, 38, 39
"Suicide Squad," 35

T

telescopes, 6, 16, 17, 20–21, 27, 28
True History, 33
Tsiolkovsky, Konstantin E., 22–26, 34, 36

U

universal gravitation, law of, 18–19
Uranus, 20, 24

V

Venus, 11
Verne, Jules, 23, 33
Virginia, University of, 28
V-2 rocket, 34, 38

W

War of the Worlds, The, 29, 33
Wells, H. G., 29, 33
Williams College, 28
Wright brothers, 28

Y

Yale University, 28
Yorick, 38